BLACK

LEMONADE

poems

Black Lemonade: ~~Poems~~

Copyright 2015 by Lawrence D. Benson

Published by

Miras Press
PO Box 581671
Minneapolis MN
55458

ISBN: 0-9823569-3-5
ISBN 13: 978-0-9823569-3-7

www.miraspress.com

Cover Design by Lawrence D. Benson

Image Crop: "Stowage of the slave ship Brookes under the regulated slave trade act of 1788."
Library of Congress Prints and Photographs Online Catalog.
http://www.loc.gov/pictures/item/98504459/.

Black Lemonade: ~~Poems~~
LAWRENCE BENSON
Miras Press/Minneapolis

To captives every-when and everywhere;
in all shapes, sizes, and colors;
of others, constructions, and ourselves.

FOREWORD

I wonder about destiny, the idea that there are situations, some would say, lives, that are already out here for us, Awaiting. This includes the notion that choices made for us, and then by us, are always the right choices en route to the life that awaits. My mother made a choice to have a baby at fifteen, which, after pregnancy, placed her in the position of having to make other choices: Would she deliver the baby she was carrying and become a fifteen year-old mother? Would she marry the man with whom she got pregnant? After these choices came others, the least of which, seemingly, was whether to move into a downstairs bedroom and give up a raggedy pair of bedroom slippers; or, consistently risk falling, jeopardizing her life and her unborn baby's life, my life. It was her choice to not give up the slippers and stay upstairs, recounted by her to me, that I perceive, to a degree, as apparently influencing my life, body, and the emotional bond with my mother that partially shapes me.

The trauma and turmoil that was locked in my body suggests that, though still confusing and painful, her choice of falling ultimately saved my life, stored this and future trauma in my muscles/fasciae, and enabled me to stay/float in the space caused by unstitched muscle. This, in turn, allowed me to not be completely overwhelmed by being—for lack of a better word—human: breathing, poor, male, b/ Black, traumatized, discursively covered over as either a norm or "an exception." However, the resulting disconnected feeling was so distracting that it ultimately consumed me and my journey, an attempt to connect/re-connect/claim/reclaim my body and my self in the face of trauma. Again, all choices in which I seemingly had no choice, choices made by my mother, father, their families, Authority relative to Slavery and America, me, school administrators, people with more power who demand access to our bodies.

Fast forward to my experience of my ability to "make my own choices," and then to the ultimate realization that many of those choices, if not all, were driven by things of which I had no control (because they are Needs): desire to connect to mother, father, country, planet; to feel safe, compassion, alive; to be gently touched.

The lemons, those bitter, uncontrollable things, squeezed me: my eyes, brain, throat, pelvis, lungs, heart. All of these things I had to revive, breathe electricity, energy, ME, back into. So, I turned inward, in a manner of speaking, imploded. I was not sure if I possessed the courage to withstand the onslaught of experience, but I was sure I had the curiosity. I had wondered if a stranglehold was my destiny, if going through life barely breathing was my path, knowing that if I gave up, what I had perceived about life and gods and infinity would be true, that they are perverted, bizarre, and malevolent—only.

Of my collections of poems, these poems connect most intimately to my current, most grounded yet fleeting experience of myself. Squeezing these uncontrollable things, these lemons, I do not mind if the acid burns my temporal cuts, psychic wounds. It does not matter if the meaty pulp squirts in my eyes and beckons tears. It does not matter if the bittersweet juice draws my lips in tightly. All that matters is my curiosity.

Lawrence Benson
December 10, 2013

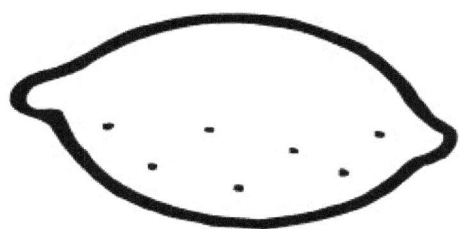

ACKNOWLEDGEMENTS

Slaves

We   J.L.

Disconnected   Family

Traumatized   Friends

Bodies

CONTENTS

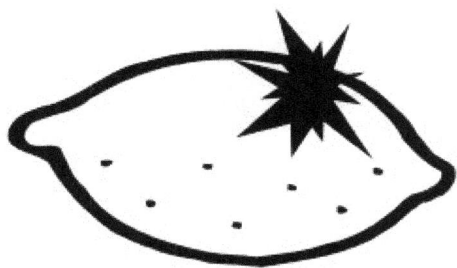

When life gives you lemons, make . . .

Black Lemonade

I've all these lemons
biting my tongue
with acid teeth
        drawing my usually hesitant lips
        into convulsive tightness,
but, what color, the Juice?

Will it be the color of day
citrified—
orange-y and lemon beatings of warm
gliding through you?

Will it be clear like water
purified—
relieved of pulp,
no residue?

Maybe shades of pugilized hearts
traumatized
by constant deep poundings
actualized black and blue?

Perhaps
becomes all and one
realized
the essence of the light
that flows through the fervent juices
the color of deep dark night.

Stalled

(the making of the moon)

Older boys and grown-assed men
had their hands down my pants
way before I was ten:

Could it possibly be they all saw
the Clear Blue© writing on the wall,
the violation in the stall
revealed right there and then?

As I fled home not knowing why
or what just happened, I tried to cry
but could not, so I decided to fly
outside of myself never to return.

Observing me each second higher
I rose objectified, further from fire;
embracing coolness I became the liar,
but I will never forget the Burn.

Sweet Subtle Sublime

Wretched encounters,
      situations
        hiding our Untidiness:
            lust,
            desire,
            notions of turmoil
revolving—
elegantly gathering answers,
recording death,
truth,
how everything assumes being
sours, eventually, narcissistic candy
(essential or forbidden?)
lightens illicit memories innocence
took,
smiling as smoldering fire
reveals estranged eyes
        dying
        omniscience
me.

S   S   S

W   e
          s
          h   o   U
                    l
                    d
                    n   o   t
r
e   g   a
r   d
t
h   e   a   b
s   e   n   c
  e   o   f
l   i   m   i
t
s   a   s   f
r   e   e
                    d
                    o
m .

Umm, Delicious!

I got my black boy bravado
in the midst of a white smoke dream
luscious
deep cherry visions swirl
with richness from my blackberry cream.

The melanin, it called me in
flared my nostrils with your smell,
while harmonic, swirling winds
extract sweat from where heat dwells.

That sexyassness that rides your voice
ooh, it drives me wild
back to the jungle
where my blood first boiled
as savageblackAfricanchild.

I confess, your breasts
are above the rest
simply, no one can deny
the moments you caught me
caressing them
with octopussian third eye.

And even though
I can go
on and on 'bout yo' behind
I would rather skip to the bestest part,
right to dessert, your mind.

911

(for one, me/us, Eric, and Osama bin Laden)

OPERATOR:	"9-1-1, Operator."
ME/US:	"Yes, I need help. We need help."
OPERATOR:	"Calm down. Slow down. Now, tell me what's happening."
ME/US:	"Somebody's blowing up my/our world."
OPERATOR:	"Oh, shit."
ME/US:	"What?"
OPERATOR:	"Oh, uhm, I mean, can you see the suspect?"
ME/US:	"Vaguely."
OPERATOR:	"Enough to describe?"
ME/US:	"Well, uh, he looks jealous and angry."
OPERATOR:	"Sounds familiar."
ME/US:	"So, you've heard of him before?"
OPERATOR:	"I used to be him (pause) but, anyway, keep going."
ME/US:	"I/We don't feel safe."
OPERATOR:	"Now you know what it feels like."
ME/US:	"Excuse me?"
OPERATOR:	"Uh, keep going, Honey, you're doing good."
ME/US:	"And I'm/we're angry."
OPERATOR:	"And you want somebody to pay, right?"
ME/US:	"Yeah, because . . . (pause)
OPERATOR:	"Because what?"
ME/US:	" . . . because I'm/we're afraid."
OPERATOR:	"Oh, you mean because you don't want to die?"
ME/US:	"No, because *now* living is the harder choice."
OPERATOR:	"Think about it, Honey. What's so new about *that*?" (pause)
ME/US:	"Oh, well, I guess . . . nothing." (click)

I Spend My Days Unwinding

I spend my days unwinding
from the night's contorted slumber
which, I am now finding,
has slowly colored me number.

The things that need me minding
under covers of conscience sleeping
have gathered in close, the binding
of self to self, the weeping.

In my eyes, the sunlight, blinding
with intentions much too shallow;
the time for never-minding
is writhing in the gallows.

When I draw in tight, protection,
and my bones crack out, reminding
that in patterns come direction
so, I spend my days unwinding.

Construction

Who decided that 7 a.m.
was this "magical" time of day
when early birds snatch weary worms
fly off their feathered-ass way?

'Cuz shocking my unsuspecting body awake
so as to break the fast,
is a tired throwback to chores before four
(antiquated longings of the past?).

Now there are microprocessors
jolting you to wake
brewing mountain fresh coffee, while you shower aria
to Day-Glo enthusiasm, rather fake.

'Cuz there're three or four hours left in you
and it is my confident hunch
that you would rather rest your mind's behind,
serve that early bird's ass at brunch.

Vlad the Impaler

You want them
to become Dead for you:
      pound the night
with heavy hands
and large pronating feet,
      sweep
across dingy air
using the sensitive tender area
where fingers and toes root
to search out hot Life,
      gouge
sensuously the secret shadows
that fall
on stately and vulnerable necks.

      They broke her heart
      then drank its blood
      Mercy Brown survived the flood
      dousing her eyes
      with steamy black mud.
      Mercy Brown.
      Mercy.

Under your charming spell
your infected army
      roamed countrysides for comfort
aware of the dark danger
clouding vision
unaware
that they had already been Taken
that demons burned

through their lukewarm veins
and all that remained
was the final blow
    or penetration
        or kiss.

They broke her heart
baptized in its blood;
Mercy Brown survived the flood
evading her eyes
with repentant black mud.
Mercy Brown.
Mercy.

Blackdar

(the danger of Seeing)

Life is dangerous
for boys with eyes like yours
'cause the ones who can see you
          Them—
          warm, wide open
          rolling around
have seen themselves
          lustful and eager to please
and sometimes turned away
from their reflection in yours;
          in you
being able to See
always means being able
to be seen
          similar
          familiar
          familial
and it is that
          family
          a place to (Be)long
          someone to be Home
which our Eyes have sought;

now, face to face
eye to eye to eye to eye to eye,
          I welcome
the opportunity of
          holding you in my mind,
the honor of
          wrapping you in my arms,

the danger of

Seeing.

Mother's day 2001

the Distance will commit me to growth:

by pressing my body against yours
                    I hoped
to bring you back to utero
where you had
yourself
been company and companion.

In your neutral eyes I was warm
            afraid and lonely
separated.

as space drew close
recognition enveloped us
the force of fields and Longing
                squeezed out
        collapsed
imploded
as to reveal contour

developing Body.

The Needs

(Well, look, uh . . . I know some of you will see this series, maybe all series, as a ploy for filler. You may not be completely wrong. However, this series was constructed as a necessary confrontation en route to a somaesthetic orientation. It's just a bonus that they came to me as short pieces. So, read and reread them, and take them seriously, OK?)

Need

I don't want to be a writer
I just need to write
of the various shades of darkness
thrusting my mind deeper
into night.

Need Ia

I don't want to be a writer;
I just need to write
of the various shades of darkness
thrusting my dreams deeper
into night.

Need 2

I don't want to be a singer
I just need to sing,
unleash the passion of my chords,
let my steel heart ring.

Need 3

I don't want to be a dancer
I just need to dance
twirl in the fever, heat my body
relive the tribal romance.

Need 3a

I don't want to be a dancer
I just need to dance,
twirl in the fervor, heat my body
relieve the tribal trance.

Need 4

I don't want to be an actor
I just need to act,
contradict mediocrity,
and preserve duality's pact.

Need 4a

I don't want to be an actor
I just need to act,
validate mediocrity,
and preserve duality's pact.

Need Workspace

Validate	Mind	Dreams
dreams	passion	mind
relive	fervor	fever
contradict	validate	relieve

Passion	Fever	Relive
dreams	passion	mind
relive	fervor	fever
contradict	validate	relieve

Fervor	Relieve	Contradict
dreams	passion	mind
relive	fervor	fever
contradict	validate	relieve

Being Rocks!

Boisterous Black   Babies   Brandishing Boombastic
Empathy,   Ecstatic—   Enraptured— Expelling   Effervescent-like,
Irrationally Irresistible Instances,   Iridescent   Illustrations,
(Naturally Natalitic?) Negotiating Neurotic   Navigations,
Gracefully Growing,   Granting   Gilded   Giving   ROCK.

Pool

I did not know what was in stored
when I fell into your eyes
I had already grown too accustomed
how love feels when it dies.

Your smile lit pathways through me
straight to the darkening part
decision. Decision split indecision
as to the opening of my heart.

Dial tones became discordant
they clashed with shallow breaths
as your rumbling voice released my head
like I had lived a thousand light deaths.

Chance meeting: tentative communion
Love Shuttle Endeavor zooms
to orbit in infinite infinity
amidst the cosmic booms.

Where we can let our heads ring high
let auraic guards down low
as universal resonance washes through
and love begins to grow.
                    (again.)

Sometimes . . .

Sometimes, when I am just sitting around listening to music,
I remember how "black" I am;
how Music evolves from my cells,
frenetic yet controlled movements
               mistakes and longings
move my chocolate body
        semi bitter sweet
in ways I have long since forgotten,
though I had once mastered
some would say
even Become.

Sometimes when I am, just sitting around, listening to music
I recall how black they said I needed to be
in order to Be
black enough to deserve the insult,
though knowing that I *was* the Insult
I opted for the present.

Sometimes when I am just sitting around listening to music
I reminisce how black I used to feel
when the beat moved my eyes to the Inside
so that I could not see the ones on me
                    raping me
as I made love to bass lines
and soulful syllables
grooving and gliding
through me.

Sometimes when I'm jus' sittin' 'roun' lis'nin' t'music,

I am Black.

I *am* Black.

I am Black?

. . . *I am Black.*

I Like Getting Drunk and Dancing

I like getting drunk and dancing;
yes, you know it's true.☺
I like getting drunk and dancing
(in circles)
to rid the memory of you.

Yeah, sometimes I get lonely,
ascetic bored and blue;
I speye the bottle, clink the glass
'cause there's nothing else to do.

I look to the sky
with cran and Skyy held high;
Oh, what a splendid view
of the world in my eyes
and me in the mirror, wondering
if I ever had a clue.

I've run out of lime
in the nick o' time
yet again, nothing is new
through goggles of grain
when you saturate your brain
start humming that tune on cue.

Michael or Prince or Culture Club,
Janet or Tina or George,
Sade, Robbie, Natalie singing
of paths I have yet to forge.

Because in my body

the dance was locked
(And my muscles? Oh, so tight!)
by things of which I had no control:
hands molesting me at night.

When the buzz creep creeps upon me,
in me over me through,
I dance, I dance, I dance in circles
'cause I remember you.
(I do.)

Janine's Mirror

Joy and laughter are becoming you;
and there is a place,
nurturing time, that wants,
illuminates hallowed imperfection
negates the
end,
eventualities,
nakedness and
imagination;   the ultimate
nothingness that terrorizes us
anxiously tugs on our freedom
justifying the notion that we are.

J
a
n
i
n
e
e
n
i
n
a
i

The Absence of Milk

I dive deep into your darkness
at night when I can't sleep,
disturbing rouge waters:
pooled bloody tears; I weep

when you look at me. I see it,
the burning abyss from within
reflecting strong, right dead at me
to commit what we call sin.

The breath I move is heavy,
tumbles 'cross 'lectric tongues
that dart with fire to unlock
caged butterflies in my lungs;

they flutter when you are near me
swell my sunken chest
which only gave way to darkness
so the light could rest.

My Beloved Delaware

Nothing can compare
to the air in Delaware;
'cuz this is where my nostrils opened,
stole my first moist breath on a dare
to flee the place so comforting, sure.
Raggedy slippers on the slick wood floor,
she would always cause a ruckus; pregnant,
wobbling at the fourth or fifth stair,
then BLAM! right to her tuckus.
More shaking, tumbling, than ever before,
bulwarked feet
'gainst vagina's door,
she pushed and pushed and pushed some more
while I deprived myself of air.
Hold it, held it, holding my breath
as they fought to get me out,
refusing to breathe 'til he smacked my ass,
forcing me to shout
and take it in, took it in,
the dank moist swampy air,
that permeates like a heavy wet fart
in my beloved Delaware.

Illusion Of Arms

Echoes of your arachnid past
have crawled upon you and now, at last,
the feeling of disconnectedness
and space between your bones
is fading, subtly, into moans
that rumble around your belly and back
to your heart, your cock, your spine and crack,
firing something serpentine
curving, roughly, into line.

Blue Room

No One matters as ticks tempt evolution;
rather we hide all that hate
and perilous pennings evoke,
never soothing time or mastering eternity.
I walk in life, lavishly.
        As love wastes away,
your sullen, haunting,
amorphously vacant eyes
thrust, hurriedly, in so deeply,
enticing empathic proddings beneath lust,
under evil.

Resist.
        outmaneuver.
        overcome.
move.

No matter what happens to me I will Always have this deep blue Room.

Finished in Vegas

black skin brown skin
Indian 'poose
suckling firmly on Nipple
afraid to let loose.

black skin brown skin
Indian child
deadening yourself
to the call of the Wild.

black skin brown skin
Indian boy
trodding through life
as a white man's toy?

black skin brown skin
Indian man
forgetting those Hands
just as fast as you can.

black skin brown skin
Indian being
now it makes sense,
" . . . in circles comes Seeing . . . "*

* This line refers to my poem, "Scrambled," which deals with questions of conception, movement, and circle energy.

The Fire Chronicles

(Okay, definitely filler.)

The Fire Chronicles

The fire chronicles
the Heat and the warmth signals
the ageless summer.

The Fire Chronicles Ia

The fire chronicles
the Heat and the warmth signals
the aging summer.

The Fire Chronicles II

The fire chronicles
the Heat and the heat signals
the aging summer.

The Fire Chronicles III

The fire chronicles
the Heat and the heat signals
the ageless summer.

The Fire Chronicles IV

The fire chronicles
the Heat and the warmth signals
the ageless summer.

The (Blank) Chronicles (#)

The (blank) chronicles
the (blank) and the (blank) signals
the (blankblank) summer.

slUg

I kissed your belly in a dream
and as wrong as it may seem
I can't wait
to drift asleep
kiss your belly in a dream.

I rubbed your head in a dream
and as right as it may seem
still fight or flight
can't wait 'til night
to rub your head in a dream.

I gazed your eyes in a dream
and as wrong as it may seem
began to melt
by what I felt as
I gazed your eyes in a dream.

I have longed for you in a dream
and as right as it may have seemed
I must continue to fight
until the light of day
(too long) for you.

Oh, I Was Prehensile

I slinked down into my basement
sneaking upon my self
fragmented
uncoiled
lovingly misshapen
cold and damp on a shelf.

Moving On

You no longer get to witness
be privy to those places
deep dark damp in my basement
where I hide my true sex faces.

Those grimaces grunts and growls
that I fought to hold in stasis
grew stronger, more grueling when
you rounded second and third bases.

Home glared in your eyes as you fixed on the prize
snug up against my spine,
igniting the supple tenuous curves
into smooth electric line.

Now it's humming blending fire
metamorphosing to air
to space to breath to nothingness:
not the not not of being there.

I'm cooling now, coming back,
falling into graces.
I'm older now but younger now
by shedding all the faces.

About the Author

Lawrence Benson writes.
He is in Minneapolis, everywhere, and nowhere.

www.ingramcontent.com/pod-product-compliance
Lightning Source LLC
Chambersburg PA
CBHW060422050426
42449CB00009B/2078